BIG CATS

Written by Tamara Lubic
and Barbara Peacock

This cat is **little**.

Some cats are **big**.

This is a **tiger**.
Tigers have stripes to help them hide.

Can you find the tiger?

These are **lions**.
Lions live in a pride.

Boy lions have a **mane**.

A mane is thick fur around the neck.

Here is a **jaguar**. They have spots.

The spots are shaped like roses. They are called **rosettes.**

Jaguars like to swim and fish.

Here is a **snow leopard**.

Snow leopards
like the cold.

Snow leopards can jump as far as 50 feet!

Look at it jump!

Tigers, lions, and jaguars **roar**.

A lion has a very loud roar.

Can you roar like a lion?

Snow leopards do not roar.
Snow leopards **purr**.

Can you purr like a snow leopard?